Dirt Road

Kerry Moyer

Press   Topeka, KS

Dirt Road
Copyright © 2019 Kerry Moyer

All rights reserved. No part of this publication may be reproduced, distributed, or transmitted in any form or by any means, without prior written permission of the publisher.

This is a work of fiction. The names, characters, places, and incidents are either a product of the author's imagination or used fictitiously, and any resemblance to actual persons living or dead, business establishments, events, or locals is entirely coincidental.

Published by Kellogg Press
Topeka, KS 66606
kelloggpress.com

Printed in the United States of America

Curtis Becker, Project Manager/Copy Editor/Layout and Design/Cover
curtis@curtisbeckerbooks.com

Photos by Kerry Moyer

Author Bio Photo by Corky Heller
chellerphotography.com

ISBN: 978-0-578-44617-2

Library of Congress Control Number: 2019900267

Dedication

I dedicate this book to my wife Sarah and our boys Edward and Miles. I would probably go off the rails if I didn't have the three of you to keep me grounded. Thank you all for putting up with me and all of my madness. I love you all with all I am.

To my dad and the life he could have had if things had been different. He is woven into the words of this book. When he died, we were friends. I am glad we had that.

I

Let's Start with That	3
Mud Pies & Valentines	4
Ketchup Packet Soup & Other Tenement Apartment Cuisine	5
If Things Get Bad	6
Throwing Hay	10
Violence	12
Red	15
The Pocket Knife	17
Sitting in the Bar with Nothing Particular To Do	19
Praise B & Pancakes	23
Duke	25
Sunset in the Flint Hills	27
The Windmill	28

II

Moline	32
The Mailbox	34
Phoebe	36
Michael Kevin	37
Carpets	39
Toast	40
My Brother	41
Between	43
Porch Sitting	44
Aerial	45

III

Four Bottom Plow	55
Blue Ribbon Lawn	57
Weeds	58
Stuff	59
Strings	60
Looking Out	61
Forgetting	62
Death Fiction	63
He Is a Shade	64
Lord	65

IV

Running	69
Waiting	71
A Father's Heaven	73
Boyhood Things	74
Edward James	77
Night Fishing	79
Willow	81
Breakfast	84
The Scene	87
Broken Pottery	88

V

The Mirror	91
Old Bones	93
I Drift	96
Driving with Corgan	97
The Good Pastor	99
Exit Wound	100
Pain	103
Rage	104
Jingles: And End with This	105

Some beautiful paths can't be discovered without getting lost.

Erol Ozan

I

Let's Start with That

My dad was a clown that drank whiskey
from a foam sandwich
You wanna ask me why
I've walked this tight rope...let's start with that
and then he made us do it
Put on the wax clown mask
and smile
Dance around and hand out candy to
kids
like me
and they knew
Me
and the drunk clown
Balloon animals, birthday parties and the heat
the makeup
Hellish paste with itchy wigs
and no fun at all for a seven year old

Kerry Moyer

Mud Pies & Valentines

Anna on the corner
played in mud
Meticulous builder of pies
mud and earth, shaped Valentines
Walking awkward and eyes rolling
unlaced shoe strings
patched blue jeans
at seven strolling past
Mud Pies and Valentines
We played
shaping our dirty earthworm dough
Muddy kiss on the cheek
mud caked on crossed, nervous feet
kitchen behind the hedge
plastic bucket
plastic shovel
all the laughter
two kids could hope to have
while mud was still a friend

Ketchup Packet Soup & Other Tenement Apartment Cuisine

If you take four packets of ketchup
packets from the crisper drawer,
packets sitting among mustard packets,
packets, packets galore
If you take those ketchup packets,
open them and squeeze the red ketchup
into a bowl
and warm tap water
a little table salt and a pinch of pepper
Stir with a straw or plastic fork
Garnish with stale saltine crackers
You have something to eat
with a ten-year-old's imagination
and appetite
After a day without,
it is tomato soup and crackers
What child doesn't love tomato soup and crackers?
Soup and crackers
sugar water to drink
A fine meal indeed!

Kerry Moyer

If Things Get Bad

I watch him shake
Tears and snot draining from his face
between halted broken sobs
He begs me
find some beer
telling him I don't know how
telling him to just pray
Two cushions away on a trembling couch
he speaks again
begging and crying
hands reaching
retreating
flipping
flopping
floundering fingers
I shrink and slip into the crack between
cushions: dust, bits of trash, and loose change
The twisted shivering mass
collects himself for a moment
Could you go find some?
I'm twelve
Mind goes to the creepy-looking man two houses down
The drunk black lady who sat on the porch smoking
Jittery
It was dark
I can't leave
My little brother Danny
crying and scared
climbs into dad's lap and slides off
climbs again
Dddddamit!
Danny shrinks away
moving into the hallway

Dirt Road

I call out to him to stop
he doesn't need to see anymore
Grabbing a Bible and reading him verse
telling dad he will be okay
and he shakes
and cries
and shakes
and breaks
For a moment he eases
then it builds again
scared,
helpless

I hear a knock on the door
It's late and it's a poor house
dangerous neighborhood
but I answer
A tall well dressed Asian man in glasses
I remember him
kind
proper
a reassuring smile
I don't remember his name
I wish I did
He walks in
two sacks of groceries
states softly,
"I was worried about your dad and you kids"
I follow him to the kitchen
Danny pokes a head in from the hallway
The man places the brown sacks
onto the counter
pulls two six packs of Milwaukee's Best
deliberately from one sack
puts one in the fridge and disappears with the other
I walk out to see

Kerry Moyer

Dad sitting on the couch
smiling
Pathetic halted thank-yous follow
The tall Asian man hands Dad one of the six packs
a quick pat on the back and back to the kitchen
The second sack held bread
glorious, beautiful bread
and ham
reddish, pink ham
a new shiny white gallon of milk
"You boys eaten anything?
I don't see any food"
I pause--
It has been two days
I tell him
"We ran out"
Leaving his phone number
on the kitchen counter
next to the beautiful bread
he says,
"Call me if the food runs out
...Or if things get bad."
Looking over the top of silver rimmed glasses
again a pat on the head
Long strides
the front door shuts
and I make a sandwich
pour some cold delicious milk
While Dad sits quiet
still
I hear another can open

Dirt Road

Kerry Moyer

Throwing Hay

At sixteen, I am strong
throwing alfalfa bales
stone grip on twine
in dusty rectangular stacks
God-awful heat
pouring over everything
running sweat down
into burning, squinted eyes
dripping on dusty muscled arms
The barn
galvanized, gray burning box
surrounding the rising stacks
built with strong, youthful backs
in our furnace

John was slow and looked tired
bale is snatched
from gloved hands
he is sent down
to help feed the conveyor
The shame in it shows
on his face as he scrambles
down to the waiting machine below

At sixteen, stacking hay
a farm boy's race
but for the occasional snake
or one cut in half
that stops a reaching hand
mice scurry from cracks
making sport for the calico barn cat
with her round crying kittens
fat from cows cream

Dirt Road

wondering around the barn floor below
not far from mother's care

We tilt red Coleman jugs
feeling the cold stream
then another bale to seat
until sundown
when we climb down
from the stack
and hear the call:
Myron the dairy farmer
hollers
See you tomorrow, boys
when we will return
to stack
a few more bales.

Kerry Moyer

Violence

Blackened eye,
flying spit,
hair twisted in a vice like grip,
tan, leather jacket
christened red,
A Bloody
Damn Mess.

And the flames pump
through him with
pride and rage and between
pounding swings and words:
DON'T EVER
HIT ME AGAIN

And again,
splatters of red
split lip
dripping sweat
skin hanging from cheeks
a tooth lodged in the left ring finger.
Lefties have an edge
A Bloody
Damn Mess.

Bloody tears roll,
for a moment he sees,
feels, fears,
Power
Beaten, broken,
his body falls

Dirt Road

Big Danny Cook
drags him back to the gold
Olds Cutlass
"I'm getting a gun"
The words come, slurred and dripping
rage
shame

The Cutlass screams away

Numb at seventeen
but strong,
focused

Wichita PD pulls up and the blonde,
mustached officer asks,
"Is everything alright?"
A muttered half truth, "Everything
is fine, officer."

The car pulls away, slow,
unsure
A tan, blood-spattered jacket turns back
exhales
slow
deliberate steps
back to the tenement apartment
to wait;
A crying younger brother looks on
framed
in a dingy square window

Kerry Moyer

Red

I remember
brown, dancing eyes
red-lace lines
touching strong fluid hips
hotter than the center of my sun

You
pulled the air straight from
the middle of every exhale

You
stalked around the bed
and I couldn't breathe
collapsing into myself over and over

You

My fingers found
fire
and all the stumbling touches
fingers at seventeen could find

I fell
Dropped from miles above the Earth
Landing in the flame
That would consume me for three years

You

I only said it once
quiet
exhaling the truest thing I had ever said
when you were still,

Kerry Moyer

    sleeping in my arms
    A million moments later
    I wake up
    tangled
    wrapped in sheets
    older and with the heart of a boy
    but for the moment
    I remember
    smile a sweet sad smile
    then drift back to sleep

The Pocket Knife

Grandpa Jim carried a three blade Stockman
A tool he would use for this or that
around the house
to cut string
open boxes
pry an occasional nail
open the mail
He'd broken a tip
prying something stubborn
like him
He lost it one time
in his shed
but found it again.
In good times,
the scales were cracked
dropped on the concrete floor in his shop
and bounced next to a box
filled with oily nuts, bolts
random sockets
and with a head shake and grin
slipped it back into his pocket

Over coffee
shortly before he died,
he reached into his pocket for his knife
for what would be the last time
slid it across the table to me
said it's yours now grandson
it's been a good knife
I don't think I've owned a better one
With its dark patina
cracked scales and broken tip,

Kerry Moyer

    a useful gift
    from a man I miss

Sitting in the Bar with Nothing Particular To Do

The blonde, lacquered wood is smooth
cool
My amber glass of beer
sits
1/8 of an inch of head
foamy
cold
A bluesy, smoky voice
a rhythm
comfortable seat
An older woman talks to a friend
maybe friends?
they are smiling
get up to leave

I know the guy at the other end of the bar
I always see him
He's always here
bloodshot eyes
red-faced
muttering
catches himself
looks around
He sees me
half nod
I lazily raise my left index finger from the lip of the glass
in reply
And that's over
thank God
He's always here
He always looks

Kerry Moyer

Nice guitar riff cuts through the air
I think it's louder
An attractive woman just walked in
I saw
everyone saw
I look deliberatly and smile
She sees
She always sees
a smile in return
and She floats past to friends at a corner table
they are loud
middle-aged
probably decent tippers
The bartender in me remembers
one Harley Davidson owner in the bunch
He looks clownish in his leather jacket
but he doesn't know it
Guys like that
they never
know
The attractive woman sitting there
flips long blonde hair
serving smiles
gets drinks all night
talking motorcycles

This song is going on and on
steady pulsing
rhythm
Two friends toast to something
the guy next to them salutes
Funny looks are exchanged
spare guy
stares back into his glass
His beer lacks character

Dirt Road

it's flat
warm
I've taken three drinks
it's still cold and I think
it's all I do:
Think

The song just keeps going
then stops
midbeat
on the edge of a symbol crash
My glass in the left hand mid-damn-drink
taking the rest of it down
empty
and exhale

The bartender is cute
flashing eyes and secrets
flips dark hair past auburn eyes
walks up
Ready for another?
The word wanders lazily out of my mouth
Yeah
Looking back down at the smooth,
blonde, lacquered wood

Kerry Moyer

Praise B & Pancakes

Grandma B was at the stove
pouring glorious, golden batter
into her black cast iron skillet
The faint smell of bacon grease
wandering through the kitchen
As I sat
waiting
for what I considered a gift
from the Almighty
Grandma B, with no prompting from anything,
anything evident to me,
Begins to tell the story:
The near tragic tale of my birth
and the divine intervention
Grandson, she says,
You almost died by God!
Her spatula going in motion between its brief
and purposeful meeting with the forming batter
I prayed and prayed!
I prayed for two days!
Didn't sleep a wink
Lord please don't take him...
I'd pray and pray!
She spoke the words like a Baptist preacher
voice rising and falling
eyes cast upward and then down
open to the Lord above
then closed in solemn prayer

Grandma B conducting the choir of colorfully
      painted roosters
perched proudly on plates placed above her
      altar

Kerry Moyer

    Spatula waving in triumphant reverent motion
           above
    what is now a fully formed pancake
    It was large, filling my whole plate as she sat it
           down
    lovingly, before me
    And I knew, like I always knew, every time I heard it
    I was still here because
    well...
    Grandma B and the Lord almighty...
    to hear her tell it

Duke

Playing guitar is cool
It just is
Everyone knows
the coolest guitar
Jazz
Blues
Duke has long dark dreads
which sit gloriously on his head
The music
Duke and his wares
call California home
for years
long, spiderlike fingers roll
lazily over steel strings
each word drawn out
One long velvety note
bends and wails
Hey
I kinda like that
You know, BB King only got big because
You know, white people like him
Lucille and his bellowing voice
Her distinct wail
Duke grins
reclined
the Kansas in him
can breath
Here

Muddy Waters
Coltrane
A Love Supreme
Duke's musical mind

Kerry Moyer

    Cuban Jazz
    a musical find
    I'm a farm-boy-white,
    jagged to Duke's smooth,
    deep, fluid laugh--bends
    then wails
    Metheney has good stuff
    you know
    Duke shifts
    hand moves up the neck to find the next note
    You've got that picking style
    a nod my way
    I think
    Cool
    Duke lays down a rhythm
    I walk a lead scale
    another nod
    We find the groove
    the sound
    twelve bars--
    and for a few minutes
    it's divine
    the notes being blind
    to his black
    and my white
    friends going way
    way back

Sunset in the Flint Hills

Brushstrokes of orange, red, and gold
God's canvas
setting upon tallgrass
on an evening ride
the colors crest
brilliant
bright
over flint rock roads
Gravel dust covered bikes
traveling rolling hills
punchy climbs
Friends find a line
with pedal strokes turning
clipped shoes rotate in time
stopped to gather
then off again
Miles move
rolling under turning rubber
The pace quickens
riders push
and the sun is down
Luminous line of lights
rides back into town
another ride
crushing gravel under beautiful skies

The Windmill

There is an old, rusted windmill
not far from a treeline
Wood and steel
sitting back a ways from the road
A small pond sits one hundred yards
east of it
Limestone rocks make a square
telling of a structure that had lived there

Bringing the bike to a slow stop
I unclip my feet from where they sat
placing them firmly on the dusty gravel road
Pulling my bottle from the frame
I squeeze a cool drink
thinking: who lived here?

Children in the front yard
running around the white painted farmhouse
A haggard-looking woman
Holding a fussy baby
Tangled brown hair with strands of gray
Long and falling onto shoulders
Covered by the gown her grandmother made for her--
or was it a wedding gift?
A man in worn and dusty overalls
smoking a pipe
whittling on a small gnarled stick
resting in the evening quiet
watching his children play
from a porch he built
His skin dark from working
under the sun
setting behind the windmill

Dirt Road

The same sun that sat behind it before
rust made a home upon its blades
I imagine there was a dog--
a dog that ran around the place
giving chase to things
before folks on gravel bikes gave them
something new to do

I pull another drink from the bottle,
my thoughts giving life to a place
taken by time
eroded by wind that still makes
rusted blades turn
until the same wind brings it down
to the waiting tallgrass and weeds
on the ground below
Then, who will wonder?
Who will know?

Any lives ever lived
with nothing left to show--

Beginning to roll, I clip back in
bringing me back to the road ahead
leaving my thoughts
and the rusted windmill behind

II

Moline

Yellow cast iron
caked in oil
pulled the plow
over stubborn ground
to turn damp clods upward
against the burning sun
while the engine roared
and wheels rolled
over Oklahoma
red earth

Kerry Moyer

The Mailbox

Climbing through the rusted green gate
Walking up the long dirt drive
The old farm house and buildings sit
silent and sagging
bare wood weathered
white paint flaking
dust and dirt together
bringing the whole of it closer
to the waiting ground

The boy in me remembers
running the long dirt drive to get the mail
for grandma
standing on the porch
hands placed on sturdy hips
One of many childhood trips
up and down the red dirt path

Moving into the space where
a rust red Massey Harris had slept
old empty structures
look on indifferent to me
not remembering the boy I used to be
and the house yawns through a vacant door frame
centered on the remains of the wooden front porch
grey paint making itself known
through small patches
poking out from broken boards and tangled weeds
I look into a window that once was whole
now a fractured frame with broken glass
littering the wild weeds and unmowed grass
An old recliner that I know
sits alone on a dust covered broken floor

Dirt Road

And I sigh
seeing grandpa with his pipe
resting on an Oklahoma harvest night
The silence speaks
and I turn from what is now
to go back to what had been

The buildings and brush
watch as I wander
for a little while
among memories
Moving through the years
when buildings were whole
grass was mowed
Walking back down the dirt drive
to the green gate
I glance to the right and see a post
that once held an old mailbox
Looking back to the porch
the boy in me sees
grandma waiting
hands on sturdy hips
for mail that will never come again

Kerry Moyer

Phoebe

Stretching
Feeling cool soft pressure on my cheek
Petite paw placed
Followed by a cold nose gently pressed
on my waking face
Grey fur finds its way under my hand
I yawn and she purrs in feline reply
Walking weight moves briefly across my chest
to the nightstand
where she proudly perches
before pouncing nimbly
to the dark wood dresser top above
I rise and see her in wait
Wiping sleep from my eyes I move
She gives a slow blink and quiet mew
Another stretch and I lean in
She brings her furred face to mine
to say good morning

Micheal Kevin

Why did Michael Kevin die?

Mother looks into her green coffee cup
the black liquid in gentle motion
her eyes deep and dark
Gazing
I ask again
Why did he die?

Mother looks up
dark eyes in gentle motion
Her mouth starts to move
Stops
Then a sigh
Lifts her face to meet mine
Shoulders drawn back
she speaks

He was too small
He came too soon

Mother goes back to her cup
I shift in my seat
reach for her left hand resting on the table
Mother
She looks up and her eyes are wet

I never even got to hold him
He just…
her words drift and float down
settling into the inky black
Lifting her cup
stopping it inches from her lips

Kerry Moyer

    setting it down without drinking
    Mother rises and speaks
    He went to heaven

    The words trail behind her
    as she leaves the room
    a lukewarm green cup of coffee
    sits half empty on the dining room table

Carpets

To an adult
looking down from five to six feet
the shag carpet was nothing more
than brown with random gold fibers for feet
But to the boy
whose imagination hadn't become
sleepy and stiff like dried clay
it was a sea filled with beasts
roads or streets
A place with more things to offer than
one could dream of
A place you'd never go
from five or six feet up
But the boy knew
and the little girl too
that carpet can be as much
as your imagination can show

Kerry Moyer

Toast

I rest my head lightly
upon the shock of blonde
hair sitting tangled
upon my child's head

He plays with his robot
mildly annoyed at my weight
and presence in his world

His imagination
and robot
have no patience
for me

As he turns
and asks me for toast

Dirt Road

My Brother

My brother is
stretched
Piece by piece
Straining under life's weight
Pulled to his poles

I swear to God
I hear his spirit tearing

My words
trying to wrap
around his despair

Do you have a plan?

Brother,

Don't die
today.

His fractured words
sobs

My words
measured

Just stay alive
Just for now

Live.

All your parts at war

Kerry Moyer

My thoughts running
Racing

And I breath
Remembering
I've done this before

Brother.

Calmly
my words

Just breathe.

Before your parts come screaming
at a million miles a second
slamming back into you
Collapsing
Killing your will
Sucking all my saving words into a black hole
Occupying the space where you…

Live.

I ask again

Do you have a plan?

Between

The boys were drawn into him
each toward his sides
Pulled
Hurried into place
No love in the savage arm grip
No shelter from her burning stare

Desperate, the slurred words fell
at their small shrinking feet
"You can't do that to these boys"

Rage
Pain
fell on their downcast heads
Hammer blows on small hearts
Her trap

And Mother shrank away in defeat

Kerry Moyer

Porch Sitting

Sitting on the dusty blue-gray painted porch
strong and free of the pain that tied
the weight to everything
Everything that was broken
The wounds of a fractured life
Sitting strong and breathing deep
of the Kansas air
the smells of harvest drifting lazily
through so many seasons
My father sitting, looking off into the coming sunset
white beard framing a crooked smile
gray felt cowboy hat
sweat ring holding hay dust
and prairie dirt
"You wanna go to town for a Pepsi?"

All those seasons weathered
under the burning murderous
grip of broken moments
mended with time
Grace
"Yeah dad
I'd like that"
Climbing into the old red Ford
the gravel road greets us
Heading to town
for a Pepsi
on a hot Kansas harvest day

Aerial

When I was five years old
Dad took me to fly
in a small, white airplane
red stripe running down its side
Bearded pilot with mirrored sunglasses
red ball cap
Dad lifted me up
as I finished the climb into the back
surrounded by white,
boxed in my place,
engine roaring to life
rhythmic rattle in time with my racing heart
Rolling, then lifting
pulled away from comfort
my small body floating
Nausea trading moments with weightlessness
reaching for him
Dad turns
takes my hand
with a crooked grin
tells me
"It's okay son."
Distance stretching between me and the Earth
Squares of green, gold, and brown
rolling out below like great-grandma's quilt
resting at the foot of her bed
Dad reaches back
patting me on the head
powder-blue eyes reassuring
Clouds wisping by like torn cotton balls
weightless

***

Kerry Moyer

Red-headed
red-lipsticked stewardess
pours a Coke into a small clear plastic cup
fizzing and popping over ice
Do you need anything else?

I look toward my sister
She sits gazing through thick glass
White, wispy clouds
framed
floating in blue
Her pain
moving far above the quilted Earth

***

The call had come that dad was dying
in a quiet tired voice
Flor speaks in heavy words
"You kids need to come."
Dad would brag that Flor was
a "full-blooded Spaniard"
He would say she was the love of his life:
This life

***

Fighting nausea
chewing ice from a watered-down Coke--
we descend
Voice over the intercom
We will be arriving…
leaning over my sister
looking out the small square window

a million fireflies greet us
My heart drops
knots taking hold of my stomach
Floating over gray tiles
blue walls
white lights
Busy blurry earnest faces buzzing around us
as we move heavy
toward the drawn, white curtain
eyes fixed
Gravity pulling me down
pressing breath from my chest
down through my feet
into the floor
I looked, looked again,
looked away
Eyes pulled back to him
choking back a cry
exhaling
Broken shaky grin
"My son"
The words moving
through our space
crashing into me
Fighting the panic
near manic desire to leave
Skin drawn over bone,
sunken eyes,
sunken cheeks,
shock of white hair framing the horror:
Tubes, lines
sharp snaps, clicks, hisses
pings...
I stood
sinking into the floor

again
"My son"
His tears rolling over liver spots,
and I see
will never stop seeing

Praying he would die,
machine sounds speaking:
a chorus of noise
in concert with crackling breaths

Pulling myself heavy from the tiles
moving to his side
taking his hand
kissing him
on his feverish forehead
"It will be okay"
suction tube
pulling green disease
from trembling lips

***

Dawn made arrangements for hospice care
with a brown-haired woman who said
she understood and had papers to sign
We had gathered pictures from his life,
setting them neatly in his hospice room window
He looked away
the pictures
ghosts
Framed shades of a man that had lived in a bottle
1,200 miles away
For a moment Dawn and I
framed in with everything he wanted to forget

Dirt Road

***

Going through his things late in the evening
Dawn Lynn found a box under our father's bed
a box filled with letters, pictures:
her family
Letters and pictures from when she tried
some letters unopened
no pictures in a frame
She looks up with a slight reddening of her
        cheeks
"I'm sorry"

With a slight stiffening of the back
pulling herself from the little girl
that moved through her
Hurriedly putting it all back
in her box
Closed
She slides it back under the bed
into the dark--
Dad framed on the wall
A cowboy on a beautiful brown quarter horse
Arizona sunset resting on blackened mountains
looks on indifferent

***

"I just want more time"
Dad: pleading, asking, demanding
Squeezing his hand
forgiveness
between slow labored gravel breaths
I ask if he knows Jesus

Kerry Moyer

not knowing what else to say
I tell him he won't hurt anymore
oxygen machine hissing
Dad pulling in air
fighting his shrinking, dying body
Again I prayed that he would die
sunken blue eyes
soft blue brilliance
Fading...

***

He died on a Saturday
I said goodbye in his sleeping ear over the phone
from miles and miles away
My wife and three-year-old child
needing me
home
Tired
panic attack exhaustion
not being able to look anymore
I just want more time...

Pulling away from the Earth
I wash down Dramamine with a Coke
Heavy eyes
and it all becomes a dream
Weightless

***

I was five years old
The Earth was miles below
My dad's crooked grin

Dirt Road

High in the torn cotton ball clouds
above the soft, quilted Earth

III

Dirt Road

Four Bottom Plow

Four bottom plow
shears biting
into dry crusted earth
Sits with a rusted blue frame
home for yellow jackets,
mud dauber nests
A few steps away,
row of silver discs
Red specks breaking
sheen reflecting
from a burning
afternoon sun
Chisel spiked teeth
dormant for years
Overgrown choking vines
sitting low
in twisted weeds
tires resting on steel wheels
Black rubber: cracked
tread worn smooth
miles rolled
over eighty acres
Season after season
a farmer's graveyard
weathered tools
waiting for nature
Metal's curse
pulling them down
to the ground
they used to turn

Kerry Moyer

Dirt Road

Blue Ribbon Lawn

Days roll by
since the old man collected his watch
Hung a gold-plated plaque on the wall
his wife had a stroke
hit her head in the fall
Doesn't recognize many folks
when they come to call

He goes to the market alone
grown children
stopped coming home
Sometimes they talk on the phone
but the yard is nice
Takes up hours of his time
lawn mowed, edges trimmed
by every week's end
Hoping to win
the city's "best lawn" prize again

Kerry Moyer

Weeds

Free are weeds
that grow among the grasses
Hearty, notched roots
holding deep in fertile ground
or found splitting stone
in rock choked soil
Stubborn foliage found thriving
where native flora dies
Standing bold, defiant
cursed leaves and vines
coming up between
concrete cracks
discarded top soil bags
wild things making a home
wherever rebel seeds fall
and water, sent from bursting clouds
will help them grow
while God smiles down
upon his scorned creations

Stuff

Throw all the stuff away
away from your thoughts and spaces
Throw the things away
Leave them in some hidden place
where you can't find them
Stuff we accumulate
that buries us
in debt, in sweat--
chasing, caging us
All the plastic and metal
All the bling bling chattel
Burn the damn debris
Bury the beautifully bound boxes
that hold our fat red pumping hearts
six feet deep
in the clearance aisle
Run from the piles of things
that would own you
Crush you
under a purchased pile
of nothing

Kerry Moyer

Strings

My guitar rests
on a simple black folding stand
Bronzed steel strings
run from the rosewood bridge
to nickel-plated machine heads
Solid top of battered, blonde spruce
shows years of honest use
Scratches tell of hours picking,
plucking, strumming--
of wood and steel aging
gently lifting my peace
from the place it sat
Holding the dark Nato neck
pulling it close to me
Left arm draped lazily
over the lacquered laminate side
Calloused fingertips find
frets and worn wood waiting
Breathing out from my chest
rosette circled sound hole sings
With a flick of nimble fingers
that dance over strings
and for a little while we play
Plucking my thoughts
and days cares away
until I set it down for a while
on its simple black folding stand
where it rests waiting
until we find each other, again

Dirt Road

Looking Out

Looking out my bedroom window
as light fades from day
My mind wanders to those I've lost
I think is there a way
they might still be out there
somewhere my blinded eyes can't see?
A giant reus has been played on me
Age is a lie and accidents are theater
Disease, a yarn spun by storytellers
I want to put on shoes, go out the door
travel all the roads far and wide
look until my weary eyes see them
discover that they were just waiting
for the world to find them
We would embrace
They would ask
while gently holding my face,
"Where have you been?"
We would speak of things they had missed
while the world kept turning
with friends and family in mourning
so certain we had lost them to dying
The dearly departed and I would go back
to everything they knew and life would go on
with death left on the road behind us
Never to find us again

Kerry Moyer

Forgetting

So many things
have happened
Where everyone
who was a part of it
has died
Quiet solemn march
of history
Holding hands
with the dead
who made it
Lost to memory
three generations later
Only books or films
to save them
from being lost
to time
Slipping into the dustbin
forever
without a living soul's memory
left to share it

Death Fiction

I read you had died
People writing a few words
posting prayers
stock sentiment, canned condolences
post-mortem, pious purity
goodness gaining velocity
with each pass of my pointer finger
moving over my glowing device
Pictures plastered on pages
a parade of posts procuring sympathy
prayers and sanctification
Everyone dies
Everyone dies better
My thoughts will go to you when prompted
pulled back to the small screen
notification ping and Pavlov wins again
Collective mourning like dogs to a whistle
Notifications noting your notoriety
until they stop with that last posts period
and all that momentum
collides with our human nature
and we move on
I didn't know you
well enough to eulogize
So I
plagiarize feeling
So I
can get my attention fix on the back of
death fiction on Facebook

Kerry Moyer

He Is a Shade

He is a shade
fading picture
His voice a whisper
in a timbre I no longer hear
hue of his sky blue eyes
day losing light
to coming quiet night
My father long dead
buried in layers
of passing time

Lord

Lord,
May all of my roads
see the sun
rising in the east
and setting in the west
May life's compass
find God's truth
at my horizon line
guiding me home

Amen

IV

Running

My neighbor boy runs
from his front porch
to a friend's house
four houses down
Unkempt blonde hair
wind whipped and wild
sits untamed on his head
from there he sprints
to the blue house on the corner
with dingy, white shutters,
when a young girl
waves him over

I stand in my yard
water the thirsty garden
smile and remember
being light on my feet
able to run just short of forever
swiftly soar from here to there
strong, flexed legs could spring
far on robust knees
sprint over asphalt and grass
whatever youthful legs would chance

As the evening wanes
and shadows move
over pitched roofs
parked cars in the road
I hang up the smooth, green hose
walk on worn-out legs
with miles and miles behind them
knees that creak and ache,
a sharp reminder of better days

Kerry Moyer

After a fleeting look
to the shaded street
I put the thoughts to rest;
plod inside for needed sleep
to dream of youth
and sneakered feet

Waiting

A man sits with his wife
smokes a pipe
under a covered porch;
Green metal lawn chair creaks
bent, he leans to see
who is coming down the street

Small silver and red windmill
sits centered on a freshly mowed
sea of green,
blades gently turning
in the autumn breeze

Neighbor boy
rides his new blue bike;
old brown hound dog close behind
paying no mind
as he flies by
to the bent old man
and his silver haired wife
resting in the red chair
sitting by his side

Hues of orange move
in the sleepy sky;
the man stretches,
yawns in all reply,
pats his wife's hand,
tells her it's time
to go inside,
get ready for bed

As the screen door closes

Kerry Moyer

    with a creak and a moan,
    windmill blades slow;
    The dying light
    surrendering
    to the dark of night

A Father's Heaven

Sometimes when lying in bed
my thoughts turn to time
what's been spent
what is left
how irreplaceable it is
My boys come to mind
and how they've changed
in just a few years
I see them growing
while I gray
Their time measured
with sands
through a glass
most likely larger than mine
and the day will come when I will go
close my eyes
to them and everything I know--
Pray for the heaven I've been told of
wait for them wrapped in love
and then heaven will be a place
the father in me would want to go

Boyhood Things

When I was a boy,
Saturdays were spent
in play and simple things;
fall brought new colors
to changing green

The road in front of my home
ran left to an apple orchard
where friends and I fought
the Second World War
diving behind trees
fiercely fighting
Germans or Japanese
like our grandfathers
forty years before
in places far from here
with stories too hard
for innocent ears

When apples fell
peace was found
Toy rifles silenced
for golden fruit
scattered about
We would eat our fill
until mothers called
or the setting sun was seen
casting long shadows

through the canopy
of autumn leaves

Going right the road curved;

Dirt Road

the park we'd always known
a place for boys to go
We jumped over things, raced
found spry rabbits to chase
waved at girls on swings
fought over boyhood things--
Brutal blows thrown
blood drawn red
split lips, battered grins
savage hearts shown;
giddy girls giggled
gasped and groaned

We walked railroad tracks
that crossed a rusting trestle bridge
Train whistle scream, starting gun
one hundred yard span to run
steel wheels thundered, ballasts shook
rails rattled under rolling weight--
When we reached the other side,
missile train would roar on by
our nervous laughter, shaky hands
showed those who dared
and won again

Above a calico treeline
green dinosaur smiled bright
Sinclair lights shined;
My friends and I
took meager pay
for raking Fall's remains,
pulled silver coin
from denim pockets
to spend on orange soda
in cold glass bottles

Kerry Moyer

    And another season passed--
    We sat, told stories, laughed
    in childhood's fading light
    surrounded by the places
    spaces where we grew
    and everything we knew
    was Kansas

Dirt Road

Edward James

He's a thinker
oldest son
deliberate
fingers find the keys
slow to speak
focused on the screen

"Edward James"
hearing his name
glancing up
from the glowing machine
to see his father's face,
tired from the day

The son gently shakes
dishwater blonde hair
rolls busy blue eyes
showing slight exasperation
smile forms on his face

Removing blue headphones
Edward rises from his seat
lanky arms and legs
meander over
to where his father stands
his head now reaching father's chin

Leaning in he gives
the same warm hug
he always has
The father wraps arms
around his first born son

Kerry Moyer

    Keenly aware of the exchange
    and the finite nature of such things

Dirt Road

Night Fishing

Catfish swim slow
over river rocks
worn smooth with time
Gray whiskered heads
large tails, spiny fins
move through dark waters,
kicking up silt from resting sand

Turtles rest
with necks outstretched
reaching toward
ambient heat,
perched upon a floating tree

Snakes slither
moonlight catching
slick brown scales
wrapped around
black twisted sticks
moss covered limbs

Bullfrogs bellow from
cover of cattails
peer from hues of brown
shades of varied green;
moonlight shown white
from watchful, reflective eyes

Fireflies flash,
dancing lights flicker
against a summer night sky
blinking canvas brings

Kerry Moyer

a soft glow to everything
that my eyes can see

Whoppy dog bounds out
from darkened trees
chasing things I cannot see
past the reach
of my lantern's light
while I find a place to wet a line
on the Walnut River

Willow

Rabbit died.
Lept from unsure hands
hopped and hit a tree;
fell at the boy's bare feet--
He cried, begged
"Please just move for me"
Still, white lump on green
fresh, new grass of spring

Grandpa's rule broken
cage door was opened
the new born babes
led the boy to look
gaze and wonder,
New life caged
after winter's thaw

Rabbits are meat
Grandpa said
to all of his kin
cheap to feed
easy to raise
damn good to eat,
not meant to draw
children's curiosity

Lifeless form held--
watching an old screen door
knowing he'd been warned before
about the willow tree
within the fenced backyard--
deep voice
broken haunting still

Kerry Moyer

ended his somber vigil

The boy placed his burden
in large, wrinkled hands
walked a long walk
to where slender switches sat--
Made his way back
for God's divine justice
Grandpa's corporal plan

Switch applied swiftly
Grandpa tossed the branch aside
passed the white furred mass
back to small trembling hands
opened the old screen door;
went back to where he was before

The boy stood for a time
to think, ponder, cry
decided in sorrow
A solemn service was in order
Grandma's flower garden
would have to do

small hole was made:
six inches deep,
dug with a stick--
lying by his left knee
next to pink tulips
a wild sapling;
small white rabbit placed
into quiet eternal peace:
loose earth covering
soft white fur

Dirt Road

A lone gray rock
marker found
lying still
on hallowed ground
sat gently
small earthen mound

Dirty hands folded
in reverent prayer
few words shared
for what was buried there
quiet contemplation--
boy's melancholy meditation
departed Grandma's flower garden
knowing with hard earned certainty
he would never open
the rabbit cage again

Kerry Moyer

Breakfast

Automatic glass doors open
Smell of bacon grease
floats to my morning nose
I saunter in
to the suspect glare
of grim old men
who gather for coffee
They eat biscuits and gravy
I tip my red ball cap their direction
It's met with elder consternation

Slender counter girl starts to yawn
placing a hand on her lips to stop it
Her mouth starts to form a smile
then undoes it
She speaks some words
I place a familiar order:
Tater tots that they call hashbrowns
the grande burrito
medium coffee
five sugars, three creams
I'm pretty sure I slow blink
shuffle my waking feet
to a nylon clad plastic seat

I look over my phone
unlock the screen
listen for the Pavlov
notification ping
check my messages again
post for Facebook friends

Dirt Road

Eight minutes later,
counter girl calls my number
It's about time I mumble
I had gotten restless with wonder
I rise from my place
glance around the dining space
as if some schmuck might take my tray,
greedily eat my grande burrito,
devour my golden "tater tot hash browns,"
drink my bitter black coffee--
leaving me only the sugar and cream
behind at the culinary crime scene

Lifting the tray from the tan countertop,
I move deftly to my place,
set it down before me
quickly consume
unwrapped, ever-cooling food;
take bite after salt covered bite
until the unremarkable meal is gone--
And I swear to God the burrito
is smaller than last time!
Maybe short a few hashbrowns?
I glare toward the grease-covered grill
for no less than seven seconds;
hoping the apron clad fry cook
can see my disappointment

at the lack of weight
on my brown, plastic tray

I rise from my seat,
put my phone in my pocket
grab the brown, littered tray,
walk a few feet and dump it;

Kerry Moyer

    wave to the counter girl
    who starts to smile
    and then undoes it;
    nod to the grim old men
    who throw up wrinkled hands in reply;
    then go out
    the same way I came in

Dirt Road

The Scene

I ride my bike
on gravel roads
Bikes the price of cars
hob nob with beer in the bar
Orange Strava
recording miles
Hours minutes seconds
and that next mile.per.hour.
is always at least one ride away
Facebook finds my time
pictures of shiny bikes
the next gadget
three rides of 50 miles
new middle-aged hat trick
century ride is a story
or earn the pint
all that gravel glory
Kanza talk abounds
In this dirty, gritty town
Life at 10 to 15 mph
Smiling, masculine posing
Sucked in gut
tight, bright lycra
copious collection of gear
My brand is better than yours
two wheeled top tube tribes
ready for the next
Group ride or solo roll
fundraiser cycling tour

Broken Pottery

The man was put-together
broken bits of pottery
A new creation
formed in the passions of fractured people
Cursed earthen copulation
Parents putting imperfect parts
in God's gray cold clay
from the potters wheel thrown
into Mother's kiln
Closed in hellish burning coals
white coats blinding
bright hospital lights
wiped red glaze
reflecting brilliant
blood-stained blaze
hiding cracks and dull grey
baked broken bits held in place
until heat then cold
life's savage seasons--
Stretch then shrink
push and pull
leaving the thing
shattered
at its creator's feet

V

The Mirror

Mother stood
in the bathroom
applying her face
her son standing
shaking and looking
eyes reaching
Help me

Red, swollen
black and blue boy
after Jimmy
punched
kicked
stomped
until Jimmy got tired

Her son
finding a place
for his fractured face
in the spotless mirror
taste of blood, dirt
pain and numbness
waves wash over
all the battered
bruised inches

She saw.
Magic mirror
stroke of black
applied with a steady hand
to eyelashes
Blue painted eyelids
bright in the vanity light

Kerry Moyer

Mother speaks
even
without pause

"Get yourself cleaned up"
Another black stroke
to eyes that never turn
from the mirror
and all it sees

Boy moves
toward the clean
porcelain bathtub
wheezing breaths
reaches
shaky aching hand
speckled with dried red
then silently
turns the shiny
chrome shower knob
waits while water warms
and mother finishes her face:
Spotless--
to wash it all away

Old Bones

Eugene pulled out his pipe
pushed dark brown tobacco into the bowl
and struck a wooden red tipped match
with shaky soiled hands;
gray puffs of smoke danced a ghostly dance
around a single glowing lamp

Wiping his brow with a yellow handkerchief
his eyes fell to the bucket sitting by his side
took another pull from his favorite pipe
and asked Willie Miles
what they should do
with the thing in the bucket
resting by Eugene's brown leather boot

Do we call the law?
or just talk to the preacher?
Eugene sat in wait
eager for an answer
pipe smoke collecting
like gray clouds on the ceiling

Willie Miles would have no lawman
snooping around his place.
Running shine in Missouri
when he was young
taught him that no good comes
from talking to the law
or "pert near" anyone
and finding a human bone
under your home...
well that sort of thing was
best kept from everyone

Kerry Moyer

Willie took a bite of biscuit
chased it down with black coffee
from his steel cup
and with a sigh began to speak:
No telling how it got there, Gene
and no sense in making a ruckus
now you take that there bone
put it back where you found it
cover it up and don't tell Edna
or anyone who might want to hear it;
she gets all anxious
and Miles business is no one's to know
anyhow nothing under heaven
is worth the fuss
that she will make
over that thing you found
in the ground
under this here house--
Willie pulled rolling papers from his pocket
and prepared to roll a smoke
turning from Eugene and leaving the whole of it
with his empty cup and biscuit crumbs

So, Eugene rose from his chair
and back to the crawl space he went
with the old leg bone
sitting in the bucket
gripped firmly in a shaky, soiled hand

The old bone Eugene found
was placed back into the space it was found;
the plumbing got fixed
and It was never spoken of again

Dirt Road

Kerry Moyer

I Drift

Gazing up
brilliant blackened sky
stretching out
over God's vast expanse
Stars like silver pins
like drops of glitter
above wandering,
twinkling eyes

Reaching up
fingertips tracing
the spaces between
those heavenly places
slow celestial caress
until arms tire
and I drift

Eyelids falling
sleep gently calling
lying in cool, dewy grass
covered in the soft glow
of a silver moon

Driving with Corgan

Driving down a gravel road
having dropped off a friend
at their darkened country door
headlights reflecting off of signs
posts and wire
beams stretching out
touching the edge of black

Smashing Pumpkins
playing melancholy music
from a melancholy album
Corgan's raspy whiny voice
moving out of speakers
into my pickup's cab
where it winds through my thoughts
weight of things
the day
roads, quiet desolation

An old thought
finds a familiar place
troubled man's resignation
I could jerk the wheel and find a tree
to end what just came over me

Thoughts wandering
for one country mile,
quiet train tracks crossed,
melancholy smile mustered
thinking to myself
not now
not today

Kerry Moyer

Rolling left
gray, empty highway
Corgan's raspy voice fades
making way for Mike D,
The Beastie Boys
Thoughts of sleep
and better days
just 15 miles away

The Good Pastor

Pastor stood at the wooden pulpit
scribbled scripture on white wrinkled paper
words weighted and measured
about the child who died
A smile that many in the congregation treasured
hours spent in prayer and meditation
hard, halted sobs
sober, quiet conversations
over and over for months
The good pastor
finding strength in the Son
looking out at the sea of faces
reflecting their grief at why
one so young had to die
The pastor takes a breath
says a silent prayer and begins to speak
healing words bathed in faith
about the promise of heaven and God's grace
human tears run down his face
as his eyes fall back to the page
He had written while the Lord steadied his hand
and reminded the good pastor
to trust in God's sovereign plan

Kerry Moyer

Exit Wound

Rifle sitting dusty on an old wooden rack
hanging on the tan paneled wall
five feet from the foot of my bed

I am slowly rocking,
sitting on the edge
waterbed ripples rolling,
quietly contemplating
eyes moving up and down
bobbing rifle calling
legs lifting me to tired bare feet
moving to the object on the wall

Pulling the tool down
steel-blued barrel
brown walnut stock
feeling cold in shaky hands
sliding the bolt open to feed it
a single round chambered
making it ready
to do its work--
loud clack
quiet exhale
thinking where my soul would go
how my body would fall
who my dad would call
how much red would speckle the wall--

Then the mad meditation that the shot might hurt
shaking my head at the absurd thought

Moving the barrel to its place
in front of my pained face

Dirt Road

looking into the dark round hole
with weary searching eyes--
A few seconds ticking by
I will have to pull the trigger
with a naked toe

Slipping the barrel into my mouth
scraping over teeth
metallic taste contorts my face
bringing me back
to the edge of my bed
and the state I'm in
where finding hell
or losing heaven
weighs less on me
than what I lost last week
Her
with all I had hoped we were

Then a thought comes to me
as the clanking of dishes
finds my ears
from the kitchen upstairs:
no, not now
bowing my head
putting off dying
at least for today

Resting the instrument on my lap
rising again
walking to the brown rack
putting the rifle back
leaving the round in its place
just in case
I change my mind again

Kerry Moyer

Plodding up basement stairs
pouring ice tea
taking a drink
washing the bitter
bloody, iron taste
from my mouth

Pain

I know pain
wearing wounds,
wrapping around me
script scrolling
through sorrows,
rough, scraping sackcloth,
sad shawl draping
over hunched shoulders,
bowed back
hung head
hood hiding
pained face
from the warm glow of hope--
I know pain
dancing with despair,
waiting on happiness to crumble,
pushing out light
one glowing smile at a time,
until my bulbs are burnt
broken
fractured filament,
rattling around inside
behind dark lifeless eyes

Kerry Moyer

Rage

Sometimes I feel this burning
coal of rage behind my heart
heating up hot hellfire blood
beating banging brimstone
with furious fierce fists and feet--
steaming screams
erupt from my molten mouth
I'd open my furnace
look up
and punch a hole in the sun;
big donut glowing ring of armageddon
dark and dead in the middle
my mighty, thumping pump
deafening drumming
pounding, pulsing pain
daring any thinking thing in my angry heavens
to look me in my bloodshot fire red eyes,
get me to blink
while my soul pleads to God
for his loving peace

Dirt Road

**Jingles:
And End with This***

Dad was a clown
drank whiskey
from a foam sandwich
Blew bourbon breaths
Building balloon animals
colorful crafted creatures
for raucous waiting kids

and then he made me do it
wear the wax clown mask
hot hellish paste
put on in drunken haste
with rough, unsteady hands
itchy blue wig placed
on my small bowed head

Piteous painted jesters
Parades and parties
Busy store lobbies
"Jingles" the clown
taking swigs with red oval lips
from a plastic bottle hidden
in a sandwich made of foam

*This is an alternate version of "Let's Start with That," from page three of this collection.

photo by Corky Heller

About the Author

Kerry Moyer is a community mental health case manager who lives in Emporia, Kansas with his wife Sarah, a 4th grade teacher, and their two sons, Edward (12) and Miles (8). Kerry and his wife are proud Emporia State University Alums.

Moyer is a member of Kansas Authors Club and regularly attends meetings of the Emporia Writers Group at Mulready's Pub. He feels that belonging to a community of writers is important to his craft. Moyer has published two chapbooks, "Let's Start with That" and "these boys." This collection of poetry is his first book. Readers will find that he writes about nostalgia and the rural settings he has spent a lot of his life inhabiting.

Moyer has been writing off and on since he was a teenager and credits his creative writing teacher, Steven Hind, as a major, early influence. He sees his writing as "a tool to deal with the drama and trauma of [his] early life." When he isn't writing, Moyer is a member of the local cycling community and races in many gravel grinding events, including the Dirty Kanza.

Moyer is a martial artist. He holds the rank of Master and is a 5th Degree Black Belt in Taekwondo. Additionally, he is a 1st Degree Black Belt in Hapkido and taught in martial arts for over a decade.

A modern day Renaissance man, Moyer is also a musician, painter, and leather worker.

A Note of Thanks

I want to start by thanking **Curtis Becker** and **Kellogg Press** for believing in my work and taking a chance on me. Thank you, thank you, thank you. I am touched by the trust you put in my work.

I would like to thank all of the family and friends who have been a part of my life. Each of you played a part in my story. My list is long, so here it goes.

I must start with my wife, **Sarah**, who I am certain is responsible for saving me from myself. She is the calm in my storm.

I want to thank my boys **Edward** and **Miles** for inspiring me every day and giving me their unconditional love.

To my father, **Lloyd**, whose life was a tragic mystery to me, I'd like to say, "thank you." Thank you for those moments where we connected and the hard lessons you taught me in life and death.

I want to thank my mother, **Diana**, for her moments of grace and the love she has shown over the years. Thank you for your strength during difficult years.

To my brothers **David** and **Danny**, thank you for believing in me. I want to thank my sister **Dawn Lynn**. She is a light in the world and might be the strongest person I know.

To my grandparents, who are all gone but not forgotten. Thank you for the love you gave and the memories made with you.

Thank you to my mother-in-law, **Cheryl**, and father-in-law, **Julius**.

I have been blessed with amazing friends who have never failed to be a beacon when things were difficult.

To **Kurt**, my brother, who picked me up when I was stuck in Arizona and his wife **Kim** who is my little sister, thank you for everything over twenty plus years of friendship. The two of you saved me more than once. I don't deserve the two of you.

To **Adam** for being a moral compass at times and a cherished friend and brother, thank you.

I want to thank **Steven Hind** for telling me I could write all those years ago.

I have to thank the members of the **Emporia Writers Group** for the amazing support and encouragement over the last year. **Sue**, **Curtis**, **Kevin**, **Mike**, **Tracy**, **Cheryl**, **Gena**, **Charity**, **Roger**, **Hazel**, **Deb**, **Kitty**, **Brenda**, **Becca**, **Lydia**, **Katelyn**, thank you all for your support and friendship through the writers group. If not for my involvement in the group, I would not be where I am as a poet.

To **Rosalie Krenger**, for her masterful editing and creative insight on my chapbooks, I have to give tremendous thanks.

To her husband **Josh** for listening and listening and listening over a beer at **Mulready's Pub** in **Emporia Kansas**, my adopted hometown, thank you my friend.

To **Angie**, thank you for being my dear friend and bonfied member of "my people."

I want to thank **Marcia Lawrence** and **Ellen Plumb's City Bookstore** for supporting my work and being an amazing friend to our writing community.

I also want to send out a great deal of thanks to the **Emporia cycling community** and all my "gravel grinding" friends. Thank you all for the miles and memories in our Flint Hills and elsewhere. You have all helped me "find and push my limits" over the last few years.

I want to thank anyone who ever helped me, made me smile, or was just there when I needed someone. That's a lot of people. For that I have been blessed.

Last but certainly not least, I want to thank **God** for all good things now and forever.

Praise for *Dirt Road*

Let's start with this—Kerry Moyer's poetry is at times touching and beautiful, at times jarring and disquieting, and always, always honest and story-filled. Perhaps the visual detail is what draws me most to Moyer's writing. Each stanza leaves me with a new memory, tucked into my mind's eye almost as clearly as if it were my own—the seven-year-old in a wax clown mask, a beaten face after the fight, Grandma B making pancakes, a boy playing on shag carpet. Moyer's words reveal the messiness that is humanity, reminding us that we are all grounded in love as much as heartbreak. I carry these poetic scenes with me, replaying them in my mind, enjoying the act of speaking aloud so many well-penned turns of phrase.

    -Tracy Million Simmons, owner Meadowlark Books, author of *Tiger Hunting* and *A Life in Progress*

In his debut work, poet Kerry Moyer paints pictures of his world. These glimpses of friends, family, and familiar places tell his story, but they also tell the reader's. His nostalgic lens appeals to everyone who grew up in rural America close to or at the end of a dirt road. We can picture ourselves in the apple orchard or on the porch of the old farmhouse of Moyer's youth, because we have these or something similar in our own memories. We can also see ourselves in our favorite watering hole, in trouble, and at the end of our rope. Moyer's voice becomes ours. With *Dirt Road*, Moyer introduces his voice to a wider audience and helped many of us to find our own voice and our own dirt road.

    -Curtis Becker, owner Kellogg Press, author of *He Watched and Took Note*.

Kerry Moyer, a self-described "dirt road" poet, unlocks memories of drunken clowns, hay dust, fractured people, and yellow tractors to craft vibrant images of one man's life. Moyer's verses explore the tender and the troubling: a loving grandmother's pancakes and prayers, a grandfather's gifted pocket knife, and a kind neighbor's offering of food to hungry boys and beer to a shaking, alcoholic father. Moyer paints vivid word pictures that compel you to look, that grip you and won't let go. Relish this collection.

    -Michael D. Graves, author of *To Leave a Shadow* and *Shadow of Death*

With a observant eye, Kerry Moyer writes about places he has loved - his grandparents' farm in Oklahoma, and the Kansas Flint Hills where he bicycles on gravel roads. He also writes about the sharp edges of family. While his young emotions are palpable in some of these poems, Moyer comes across more as an active observer than a childhood victim, tempering those sharp edges of family with time, perspective and maturity.

-Cheryl Unruh, author of Flyover People, Waiting on the Sky, and Walking on Water.

www.ingramcontent.com/pod-product-compliance
Lightning Source LLC
Chambersburg PA
CBHW021956290426
44108CB00012B/1089